Mommy, I Need You!

Dr. Harris

As you touch
each page & pray
that your heart will be
enlightened.

Regina C. Hall

Mommy, I Need You!

NO MORE STAINS

Rev. Regina C. Hall , MA, LPC

Publisher's Cataloging-in-Publication Data

Hall, Regina C.

Mommy, I need you : No more stains / Regina C. Hall

p. cm.
Includes bibliographic references.
ISBN 9781070993867

The author shares her experience of being sexually abused as a child and the vital role of mothers as well as other caretakers in the healing process. She provides the insight and tools needed to bring healing to the lives of the abused daughters and their mothers.

1. Child sexual abuse. 2. Child sexual abuse—Religious aspects—Christianity. 3. Child sexual abuse—Psychological aspects. 4. Adult child sexual abuse victims—Rehabilitation. 5. Child sexual abuse—Mother-daughter relationship. I. Hall, Regina. II. Title.

HV6570. H 2018
362—dc22

DEDICATION

I dedicate this book to my Lord and Savior Jesus Christ, in appreciation of all He has done in my life. I often hear Christians say, "If it had not been for the Lord, I don't know where I would be." When I think about my life and all that I have been through, I know that if it were not for the Lord on my side, my life would have been filled with lies from the mouth of the enemy.

I also dedicate this book to my daughter Amanda, who is my inspiration. I have learned many life lessons of love and determination from her. God allowing me to be her mother has brought tremendous joy into my life. I am immensely proud of the mature young lady that she is becoming. I am also proud of the fact that she understands the importance of maintaining a relationship with God. I continue to strive to be her greatest advocate. When she came to me with a problem, I believed first, researched the situation, and then determined what the outcome should be. I am not a perfect mother, but I have been a good mother.

Additionally, I dedicate this book to Mom and Dad, who were great parents and did the best they could. I have wonderful stories of a father who was an entrepreneur and hard worker. For him, education was first. My mother was an excellent homemaker who provided us with a beautiful home and encouraged us to walk in wisdom. Together, they were parents who raised us to live as productive citizens.

Moreover, I acknowledge those who are suffering, held captive by the chains of the past and in search of who they are. I acknowledge those who have been rejected, called liars, and had their hearts broken. They may see God as being angry with them and feel that they are cursed. I pray Romans 8:1-2 for them:

DEDICATION

There is, therefore, now no condemnation to them that are in Christ Jesus. For the law of the Spirit of life in Christ Jesus made me free from the law of sin and of death. (New International Version).

Lastly, I recognize those who feel there is no hope; those who believe that everyone has it better than they do, so they question why they are even living. I pray Romans 5:1-5:

Being, therefore, justified by faith, we have peace with God through our Lord Jesus Christ; through whom also we have had our access by faith into this grace wherein we stand; and we rejoice in hope of the glory of God. And not only so, but we also rejoice in our tribulations: knowing that tribulation worketh stedfastness; and stedfastness, approvedness; and approvedness, hope: and hope putteth not to shame; because the love of God hath been shed abroad in our hearts through the Holy Spirit which was given unto us. (American Standard Version)

TABLE OF CONTENTS

FOREWORD

The journey of crafting a book that will make lives better is about to be in the hands and hearts of daughters, mothers, ministers, teachers, fathers, brothers and people all over the world. Rev. Regina Hall's research, knowledge, counseling experience, and calling in ministry have equipped her for such a work as this. She has exhibited the courage to author this powerful book that can compel young people, as well as people of all ages who have been sexually abused, to understand that it is not their fault.

They are not the blame for what happened. She shares with her readers about the unconditional love of Christ and is unapologetically honest about the critical role of "Mommy." If a mother never understood how much her daughter needs her, after reading, *Mommy, I Need You!* she will understand with a fresh perspective.

Rev. Hall is a change agent by writing this book and sharing this story with the world. Your selflessness and courage to empty yourself into the work of completing the book project will offer others the chance to be released from torment and pain. After completing Rev. Hall's book, healing and restoration will begin to take place and forgiveness will be achieved for the victimized, and this is "Good News." May God bless you and your ministry, and may your book be read by many throughout the world.

Your Friend,
Rev. Dr. Mary D. Bruce

ACKNOWLEDGEMENTS

In preparing this book, there were those whose help was invaluable to me. I would like to thank my husband, Robert O. Hall, Jr., who encouraged me to press on and was willing for me to use the resources I needed to make it happen. Thank you for being my husband and believing in me. A special thanks to Dr. Mary D. Clark, who played a pivotal role in the early stages of my book by listening, critiquing, encouraging and being my accountability partner to get the book completed. You have been a special friend and have always been there to cheer me on to the next phase of my life. We have gone through so much together: divorce, single motherhood, obtaining higher degrees, remarriage, and most of all, building a stronger spiritual relationship in Christ.

A special thank you to Rev. Jeraldine Jackson, Pastor Jimmie D. Compton, Jr. (Hope Bible Fellowship Church), Dr. Jeanne Cagle (Mt. Zion Church), and the late Dr. Frederick G. Sampson (Tabernacle Missionary Baptist Church). I am so grateful for your prayers, teaching and pouring into my life during my darkest times. Thank you for adhering to the voice of God and allowing Him to use you to bring stability, deliverance, and restoration into my life. Thank you all for the countless hours spent sowing seeds into my life. I want you to know that they did take root.

Additionally, I thank God for sending me to Oak Grove AME Church where Dr. Jessica Ingram launched a third Sunday evening women's gathering. That was a special season in my life, in which God sent me to receive love from other women who hugged, encouraged, uplifted and prayed for me. In particular, two beautiful sisters blessed me with a profound sense of acceptance and love. These two women had no idea of what I was going through, and they poured so much love into me. Their hugs, love, and acceptance of me were life sustaining.

SPECIAL THANKS

I thank all who assisted me in bringing my book to fruition. For those who read my first and second manuscripts, thank you so much. It meant a great deal to have your input and insight. It was important for me to tell my story and produce quality work. I truly appreciate Dr. David Harris, Natasha Vassallo, Kimberly Burns, my husband Robert O. Hall, Jr., Donna Hicks, and Patricia Grant. Dr. Robert McTyre, words cannot express my gratitude to you for taking this journey with me, providing your expertise, listening ear, guidance, and encouragement throughout the process. Who knew that the article you wrote, "Afterword … And a Prayer" was intended for such a time as this? The alarm has sounded. My prayer is that as men read your article, it would compel many to rise and take their rightful place in the kingdom of God. Naomi Dunsen-White, your editing and content expertise brought my book into its final stretch. Thank you for sips of tea, laughter, digging in our heels and smoothing the rough patches. Your friendship and sisterhood for over twenty-five years have left an indelible print on my family and my life. Lindsey Wojcik, I love my book cover; you listened, designed, and redesigned, and a masterpiece was created. Dr. Barbara J. Brooks, your nudging and persistence gave me a deeper respect for the editorial process. The outcome is marvelous!

INTRODUCTION

Writing this book has been a long time coming. It has been brewing in my spirit for a while. Unfortunately, I resisted writing this book, allowing fear to dictate my path. The fear of no one reading my book, being overly criticized, or having my book picked apart kept me from moving forward. Isn't it amazing that fear can become debilitating and paralyzing? Thank God that I have moved beyond my fears and looked to Him for my strength.

The purpose of this book is to speak about my own experience of being sexually abused and the support needed in my healing process. Mothers are vitally important to the healing process of traumatized daughters who have had their identity distorted as a result of sexual abuse. I want every mother to know that she is needed in the restoration process. Some mothers have been wounded themselves, and are not in a position to bring healing. However, I have come to understand that you don't have to be the biological mother to be an instrument of healing in these situations. You may simply be a loving and compassionate woman with the capacity to nurture and bring healing and restoration to a daughter.

By sharing my personal story of childhood sexual abuse, I hope to provide insight and tools needed to bring healing to the lives of daughters and mothers.

ONE
Foundations

Although you may find me referencing daughter and child interchangeably, I must establish early on that from research on sexual abuse, the healing process doesn't usually take place until the child becomes an adult. Hopefully, this book will help mothers to recognize changes in their daughters and be prompted to investigate. Additionally, I pray that this book will encourage others to be sensitive to what a child may be experiencing. Take the time to listen to her words and pay attention to her body language and general behavior.

This book is also intended to serve as a resource to the surrogate. Surrogates can play an extremely vital role in the healing process of the abused. The surrogate is the person who is ready to intercede and stand in the gap. Isaiah 62:6-7 reads, "I have posted watchmen on your walls, Jerusalem; they will never be silent day or night. You who call on the LORD, give yourselves no rest, and give him no rest till he establishes Jerusalem and makes her the praise of the earth."

Surrogates: You are needed to offer prayers, hugs, encouragement, and to lovingly steer that girl away from the crippling, victimizing life that the devil has planned for her. This support includes coming alongside her, walking in the depths of her pain, and having the willingness to stay, even when there is too much to bear.

In Michigan, Children's Protective Services (CPS) is a state program that is part of the Department of Human Services (DHS). Its publication "A Parent's Guide to Working with Children's Protective Services" defines *sexual abuse* as "Having sexual contact with a child, using a child for prostitution, taking sexual pictures of a child and not stopping others from sexually abusing a child" (Michigan Department of Health and Human Services, n.d.).

1

There are more explicit definitions of sexual abuse. For instance, on Project Sakinah's website it states that "sexual abuse includes sexual intercourse or its deviations. All offenses that involve sexually touching a child, as well as non-touching offenses and sexual exploitation, are just as harmful and devastating to a child's well-being" (Project Sakinah, n.d.). Any time a child is sexually assaulted, she is also mentally, emotionally, physically, and spiritually impacted. Daughters need someone to reconnect them to the innocence of being girls. Dictionary.com defines *innocence* as "free from moral wrong." In the book, *The Trauma Myth*, Dr. Susan Clancy reports, "Many modern-day child psychologists would agree that it certainly would be expecting a lot from a child to expect him or her to resist under such circumstances" (Clancy 2011, 72). However, the child *will* carry the weight of the abuse, just as if she had committed the crime. The moral wrong has invaded her life. Therefore, she is going to have to choose (particularly as she gets older) whether or not to heal from the ordeal.

I am reminded of the scenario in the Bible when the serpent deceived Eve into eating the forbidden fruit.

> The woman said to the serpent, "We may eat fruit from the trees in the garden, but God did say, 'You must not eat fruit from the tree that is in the middle of the garden, and you must not touch it, or you will die.'"
> "You will not certainly die," the serpent said to the woman. "For God knows that when you eat from it your eyes will be opened, and you will be like God, knowing good and evil." (Genesis 3:2-5)

Here we see that the serpent deceived Eve into doing something that would change the course of her life. When our daughters are deceived into doing something wicked and incomprehensible, it also changes the course of their lives.

When I was praying about and considering a title for this book, the Holy Spirit brought to mind, *Mommy, I Need You.* I was in awe of God regarding how befitting the title. These were my daughter's favorite words: "Mommy ... I need you." She would call me for everything and anything, and at times it was nonstop. I recall one time pretending to be somebody else because she had called me so much that day (LOL!). However, jokes aside, I was happy that she called me "Mommy." It is through the eyes of God that I have come to understand that it is a privilege and honor to be called mother. "Children are a gift from the Lord" (Psalm 127:3, New Living Translation).

As a mother, I have also come to understand that a child needs to experience every aspect of what it means to be a child. I would have to say that before my innocence was stolen from me, I did have a childhood—and it was one rich with meaningful interactions and experiences.

***

The Wonder Years

At the beginning of my life, my family included my two brothers, my mother, father, and me. I can recall my father being gone a lot during the day and my brothers and me being cared for by our mother. My brother, who was fourteen months older than me, used to call me "Ding" because he could not yet pronounce "Regina." It seems that I was a curious child and I did things that my mother told me not to do.

For instance, I can recall my mother once telling me not to stand up in a chair. It was a nice, big comfy chair. I was a little girl, maybe three years old at the time. I remember her going in the kitchen and leaving me alone in the living room. When she came around the corner to see what I was doing, she removed me from the chair and instructed me not to climb back up. However, there was a tall ashtray stand that stood not too far from the chair, and it was calling for me to touch it. The only way to reach the ashtray was to stand up in the chair. So of course, I stood in the chair, attempted to reach the ashtray, and started falling toward it. My mother heard the commotion, I guess, ran in and stopped me from falling. As I think about my childhood, I admit that I was curious and constantly doing things that were forbidden.

Whether I allowed my curiosity to run amok or not, I always looked forward to my dad coming home from work. The anticipation of him walking through that door filled me with excitement and laughter. Wow! When he walked in, my brother and I almost knocked him over. He would sit us both on his lap, one on each leg, and blow air into our ears. We loved it! He would also make weird sounds on our jaws with his mouth, and we were overcome with laughter. These were regular occurrences that filled us with joy.

My parents eventually had another child, so I had another baby brother. I was not happy about it because I wanted a baby sister and she brought home a boy. One more boy ... that was all I needed. Yeah, right! I would tell my mom that she could take him back and get another one. Later on, my mom became pregnant again, and I begged her not to bring home another boy. My parents laughed at my saying this, but I meant it. Sure enough, when my dad took us to pick up my mom from the hospital, it was a girl! I was all smiles and so happy to finally have a baby sister!

The excitement of having a baby sister started to wear off after a while. My parents' friends and our family made such a fuss about her. When people came through the door to visit, they would say "Essie, she is beautiful!" So, I started telling my parents that they could take her back too. Plus, she cried a lot. I must admit though—my little sister looked like a doll. She had beautiful, curly, wavy hair and looked adorable in her girly outfits. I guess I thought she was going to be my own, personal little doll. I loved dolls, but my little sister got all the attention, and that was not fun for me.

I can remember having lots of fun playing with my dolls. Playing with Ken and Barbie were the high point of my day. Interestingly enough, Ken and Barbie are still on the market today and as popular as ever. My friends and I married them to each other and watched them kiss a thousand times. It was exciting to think that one day I would be married too and have children. You may be wondering, "What does this have to do with anything?" Well, it is the mindset of a young girl, existing in innocence, pulling from the imagery of her mind. Oh, where have those days gone? I have to say that my visions of marriage and love were less complicated than what our young girls are facing today. My thoughts were wholesome. I had the television parents of shows like *Leave it to Beaver*, the *Brady Bunch* and *Good Times* to idolize. These men and women were not jumping into bed with each other at first sight. During this time, intimate kissing was rarely shown on television. I would have to say that Ken and Barbie were married in the hearts of most girls because they were not strangers. They were in a relationship, and there was no Ken without Barbie.

My friends and I had tea parties, sipped on our make-believe tea and laughed and talked to each other. I also had an Easy Bake Oven, and we would bake small cakes for our make-believe husbands. We would say things like, "Honey, would you like some cake?" ... "Oh, okay, I will bring it right over!" I can't forget that we would also play "doctor." We would perform surgery on our dolls and bring them back to life. I enjoyed every bit of play time!

REFLECTION

Reflect on the fun of your childhood and write it down. Lord, help them to recall the good times of their childhood.

~ Reflections ~
Write Your Thoughts

TWO
The Wonder Years ... Continued

The block I grew up on consisted of married couples and retirees. It was a working-class neighborhood. Most of the homes were owned, but there were some rental homes, and single-mother households. It felt like a family on my block. All our neighbors knew and watched out for each other. Kids were expected to show respect to elders, and we addressed them as "Mr." and "Mrs." When I was about five or six years old, I noticed that my mom was often sick. Mom had problems with her gums and was in a lot of pain. Eventually, she had to have all her teeth pulled and the nerves removed. From my understanding, she had to undergo brain surgery to remove nerves. Her hair had been shaved on one side of her face, and she had a large scar. My siblings and I understood that my mother had no feeling in her mouth and she needed us to tell her at times that she had food on her face. Additionally, mom was often hospitalized, due to several heart attacks. Dad had the full responsibility for our care.

During my mom's hospitalizations, we were cared for by my dad's sister and other family members. My aunt lived nearby, and we would get dressed and run to her home when my dad was leaving for work. He picked us up after work and we would all head home together. He cooked dinner, made sure we were bathed and prepared for the next day. Dad had served in the military, and this helped him to keep us organized. I can remember him lining us up after he washed, folded, and separated the clothes for each child. We would take the clothes, march upstairs, and put them away. Everything was great, except my hair. My dad didn't know how to care for my hair. I had short, flying ponytails. I looked like Pippi Longstocking, but with short black hair. Nevertheless, I admired my dad. He was the love of my life.

A time came when Dad was no longer able to work. He had hurt his back on the job. He tried to keep working, but the pain became excruciating, and he was deemed unable to work. Even so, I watched him do everything he could to provide for the household. He sold watermelons in the summertime and also performed carpentry and roofing work. He grilled ribs and chicken, and my mom made the sides. People came all around the neighborhood to buy their dinners. Everyone loved my parents' food.

There were plenty of kids in the area, and we all knew each other. We played, fought and called ourselves "dating" one another. I liked a boy who lived on another block. He and I would find areas in my backyard to hide. We would kiss, and he would "hump" me. We pretended to have sex. Most of the kids were engaged in the same behaviors. And even though our behavior was inappropriate, it was completely innocent. It was the kind of thing that almost all children do. Eventually, we grew up and moved on to other life experiences.

The picture that I painted of my home life and neighborhood demonstrates to me that I did have childhood curiosity and a lack of understanding about what constituted a healthy relationship. I recall chasing a boy and attempting to steal a kiss. At this age, this would have been considered being a *fast* girl. I was constantly in fights in school and on the walks home from school. Even at home, my siblings and I frequently fought. I stayed in trouble and yet, I desired to be loved and looked upon with a sense of fondness by my teachers. I was fascinated by the students who were respected by the teachers and administrators. I desired to be a good child but did not always hit the mark.

Place of Wholeness: Place of pain

I had a best friend in my neighborhood. We spent as much time together as we could. We enjoyed playing with our dolls at each other's homes and her grandparents' home. Her mother and father both worked, and she and her siblings spent most of their time at their grandparents' home, which was located right next door to mine. An aunt and three uncles also lived there at the time, so you can imagine that there was a lot of traffic in and out of that house. I enjoyed being there and spending time with her grandmother because both of my grandmothers were deceased. Being there gave me a sense of wholesomeness and belonging. Little did I know that the same place that represented family, laughter, and fun would also come to represent confusion, fear, and pain.

REFLECTION

Confronting the evil may cause one to also deal with the good that they experienced in the midst of the abuse. Lord, assist them in understanding the conflicting feelings that brought both joy and pain.

9

~ *Reflections* ~
Write Your Thoughts

THREE
The Emerging Presence of God

My first experience of going to church was one of the most beautiful I have ever had. I was probably between five and seven years of age. I remember wearing a pretty dress, a hat, and black patent leather shoes with short white ruffled socks. I felt amazingly beautiful and excited about where my dad was taking us. My mom was asleep on the sofa, and I tried to wake her but I couldn't, so we left.

When I walked into the church there were so many people, all dressed up. I saw beautiful, colorful windows that I would later learn were stained glass. The church had a high ceiling— at least it appeared that way to me. The choir was seated directly behind the pastor, and they had on long, beautiful robes. I had never heard a choir sing before and they sounded angelic. As I sat there listening, I was captivated and in awe. It was not just the music, but it was about whom they were singing. They were singing about Jesus. As they sang, I saw a light shine through the window. I was so drawn to this light, that I felt it was more than just the sun. I experienced a sense of peace, and joy filled my heart. When I heard the preached Word, it was the icing on the cake. I didn't understand everything that the pastor preached, but it was clear to me that I needed to know Jesus.

When the service was over, I could not wait to get back home to my mom. She was awake, and I told her all about the singing and how they talked about Jesus. When I first arrived my mom seemed sad, but after talking about Jesus, her mood changed. All I can say is, I didn't want the feeling to end. I told my parents that I wanted to go to church from then on. I started attending the neighborhood church, Pure in Heart Missionary Baptist Church.

My mother and father didn't attend with me, so they discussed how I was going to get there. My brother, who is fourteen months older than me, was forced to take me, and he hated it. He didn't want to go, and this was a complaint of his every Sunday. However, my dad told him that he was going to go until he turned twelve years old. My parents believed that until the age of twelve, parents were responsible for the sins of their children. My parents made sure we were up on Sundays, had breakfast, and were ready to go. I couldn't wait to get there. We had to walk. I went skipping with anticipation, while my brother did nothing but complain about how he had to do this for me. He couldn't wait until he turned twelve.

It was comforting belonging to a church community. As I sit here typing, a sense of warmth wells up in me and I smile at my yesteryears. As long as the doors of the church were open, I was there. My first pastor was the Rev. Major F. Adams. He was an older man, with a gentle soul and warm smile. I recall listening to him preach about Jesus. He once surprised me by uncharacteristically shouting and dancing at an evening service. My church was pretty traditional. Before Pastor Adams brought the preached Word, the deacons would sing a bar of a song and the congregation would echo it. One verse that stayed in my memory was "I Love the Lord. He Heard My Cry." The song seemed to go on forever, but I loved it. Afterwards, one of the deacons would kneel at the altar, pray, and cry out to the Lord.

The mothers of the church sat across from the deacons. These women were older, and some had bluish-gray hair, including the pastor's wife. They prayed, cried and waved their fans. They shouted about the goodness of the Lord. These mothers represented wisdom and godliness, and they were also a support to the pastor and deacons. One particular mother left a permanent impression on me. She spoke of the blessings of God and referenced Scriptures. She would testify of His goodness and how God kept her. Her favorite Scripture was Psalm 23. Although she was a frail woman, when she spoke of God, she seemed bigger than life. I remember going home and opening my Bible to the 23rd Psalm. I believed that God was with her and I wanted God to be with me. I read the chapter over and over because I wanted to capture what it meant to her. I kept my Bible open to that page and set it on a stand. Granted, I didn't understand it at the time, but that didn't stop me. Rev. Adams became very sick and eventually passed away. Losing him was sad. Rev. Caver became the new pastor, and I recall the congregation growing. The youth usher board was established under his leadership. I became an usher and also joined the choir. I attended Sunday school, and my first teacher was the uncle of my best friend.

Unfortunately, belonging to the church community was no longer easy for me. I would get into verbal fights with others at church, and I'm sad to say, even with adults. I frequently fought with one particular boy who was the same age as me. We fought like cats and dogs. We were both sassy and were not going to let anyone rule over us. There was an older woman who was a friend of the new pastor. Boy, did we clash! She had a way of speaking to me, and I was not having it! I felt attacked by her. The other adult women would look at me with disgust and talk about me. One Saturday, the church was having a rummage sale. We kids were playing in the kitchen of the church, and I guess we were doing something this woman didn't like. She grabbed me, and we got into a bad argument. I called my mom, and she came to the church. I am not sure what they discussed, but from that moment on, my mom went to events at the church. By that time, my brother had turned twelve and was then old enough to stop taking me.

Mom eventually started going to church and built a network of friends. She was a great cook, and so were some of her friends. Every Sunday, they would cook for the entire church. You could smell the aroma of the fried chicken during service. It was hard to concentrate. Mom was well-liked by her friends, so it became easier for me to be there. The presence of my mom brought about a respectful relationship between the woman and me. The boy and I eventually made peace with one another and became friends.

REFLECTION

Think of God's emerging presence in your life and what that meant to you. Lord, allow them to see You in their lives.

~ *Reflections* ~
Write Your Thoughts

FOUR
The Turmoil Begins

In order to engage in an appropriate dialogue about child sexual abuse, it first needs to be defined. The Michigan Child Protection Law provides a working definition of what constitutes *child [sexual] abuse*. It is defined as follows:

> **Child Abuse**: Harm or threatened harm to a child's health or welfare that occurs through non-accidental physical or mental injury, sexual abuse [sexual contact or sexual penetration], sexual exploitation, or maltreatment, by a parent, a legal guardian, or any other person responsible for the child's health or welfare or by a teacher, a teacher's aide, or a member of the clergy. (Michigan Legislature 1975.)

It is important to have a framework to draw from and understand what has transpired in a child's life. What I have come to understand, is that when a child is sexually assaulted, he or she can be held captive at the age of the abuse. At one point, I thought that captivity meant that a person is confined and unable to accomplish his or her life goals. Now, I realize that a person may be in emotional prison, but still able to achieve success in life. My experience was that I was in emotional captivity, limited in movement, but still able to fulfill some of my life dreams. The greatest hurdle for me to overcome has been to gain the ability to believe in myself. As for my abuser, he was a young man who definitely knew right from wrong. He not only exploited my innocence but the innocence of his own niece. My heart goes out to every person who has been sexually abused by a family member. It is bad enough, dealing with the pain and need for healing, but to continually be in the presence of that family member just adds salt to the wound.

17

I can't recall my exact age at the time of the sexual abuse; however, I do know that I was young. By the time I had reached middle school, the abuse had stopped. I say this because a vivid memory provides my first insight of what happened to me. When I was in middle school, my gym class included sex education. My teacher showed a film about the human reproductive system. The video demonstrated how sperm is carried to the fallopian tubes and how a baby is conceived. This was mind-blowing and overwhelming for me. I sat there thinking,"Can I be pregnant?" How could I ask my teacher this question? The movie mentioned that a baby was born within nine months. I could hear myself thinking that it had been longer than nine months. However, I wondered if I could still be pregnant? I was so anxious, confused and overwhelmed, that I had difficulty keeping my composure.

I finally got enough courage to ask my teacher about being pregnant. I pretended that I was asking for someone else. The teacher chuckled but explained more of what the video meant. She explained it in such a condescending way, and that made me feel stupid and defensive. I am not sure what I said or did to cover up my feelings, but I didn't show my hurt. The conversation was brief and informative. I walked away knowing that I was not pregnant, but it was clear then that what the abuser did to me was sexual. Learning about becoming a young lady, while making sense of what my abuser had done to me, left me feeling like I was holding a loaded gun.

As I write, I now realize that my introduction to ladyhood was unfortunately riddled with confusion about who I was, in the midst of a lot of chaos. My self-image became distorted. The bickering within my immediate, extended family and community played a role in my self-esteem. My mother not coming to my defense when I told her what the neighbor had done also played a pivotal role. What the perpetrator did and said to me distorted my understanding of who I was, especially during my middle school years. I was having an identity crisis and didn't even know it.

Cries for Help

One day, my cousin was in her backyard playing musical chairs with friends, and I joined in. As we were playing, I told her, and whoever else was there, what the abuser had done. I am not sure what caused me to bring it up, but I told her. She asked for more details, teased me about it, and that was all. We continued to play musical chairs.

There was a young lady I befriended at my high school, and we talked about everything. I shared what happened, and she listened. She would even ask me questions and then listen to my response. We used to meet and talk every day after school. She was going through some things with her family, and she shared that she was also sexually abused. She was nice and fun to be around. I am not sure what happened to my friend, because I no longer saw her at school. It was like she disappeared. Throughout the years, I have shared my experience with several different friends, but the subject was never brought up again by any of them.

We live in a society in which certain circumstances are shoved under the rug, or we pretend as if they never happened. Sometimes we act as if it was not that serious. My family was notorious for avoiding or not dealing with painful issues. I learned that behaviors of this nature only create more pain and hurt for the victim. When a family does not address their pain, how can they confront the pain of the victim, that comes to interrupt the agony that they (the family) are already experiencing? They can't.

Nightmares

Bedtime was particularly difficult for me. For years after the abuse, I had a reoccurring dream. I dreamt that I was falling through my wall. The wall would open up and on the other side was a cliff with a stream of flowing water. I saw myself on the edge of the cliff, fighting not to fall in. If I lost the fight and fell in, it meant death. I did not want to die. I woke up in a panic and felt the wall in my bedroom, to make sure that it was still there. I was horrified. It was frightening to know that this was going to happen as soon as I fell asleep. Sometimes, I woke up in a sweat. This was not my only reoccurring dream. I also dreamt of roads opening up, and me literally falling through them. The pavement was always black, and multiple holes would appear, and I would fall through. Now, when I hear news reports about cars falling into sinkholes, it reminds me of my dreams.

REFLECTION

In the midst of the turmoil, Lord, show up and guide the way. Help them to find You, and surely they will discover who they are.

~ *Reflections* ~
Write Your Thoughts

FIVE
The Stain on the Dress

One day my friend and I were playing upstairs at her grandmother's home. We played all over the house—the kitchen, living and dining room, backyard and upstairs where the bedrooms were. We were having so much fun! As we played, her uncle called me to come upstairs, to where his bedroom was. We never played there. When he called to me, it seemed as if my friend disappeared. I remember not wanting to go up and my heart racing. He tried to convince me, but I refused. He sat on a step, and he pulled me between his legs. We were in his stairwell, and he made sure the door closed behind me. He coerced me to perform fellatio on him, right there in the stairwell. I could taste this disgusting stuff in my mouth, and I spit it out. After he finished his dirt, I found my friend, and we resumed playing. We never said a word. Eventually, I went home.

We usually entered through the backyard of my home, at the kitchen door. When I came through the door, my mom immediately noticed that my dress was stained. I can remember so well the color of my dress. It was a lime green jumper. At first, I did not answer my mom, and she asked again. Finally, I simply responded by saying his name. When I said the abuser's name, my mother exclaimed, "What?!" When I said it again, my cousin who was there quickly interrupted, saying he wouldn't do such a thing. I defended myself immediately, crying out with emphasis "He *did* do it!" And again, my cousin defended him. I heard my mom say, "I don't believe he did it either." She told me to go change my clothes, so I did. There was no other discussion about what happened, but I know it left a lasting impression on me. Later on, this discussion became an eye-opener. The only thing that I knew at the time was that the stain on my dress was from the abuser. I did not understand, then, that he had ejaculated sperm into my mouth and it spilled onto my dress. However, my cousin and mother appeared to have had some idea that something strange was on my dress, and it seemed alarming to them.

It's really something that we actually think we know people. We often hear on the news about how shocked neighbors are to learn that someone in their community did something horrible. In all honesty, at times we barely know the people we live with, let alone someone outside of our home. Unfortunately, my mother allowed my cousin to influence her decision to believe me about our neighbor. I have never spoken to my cousin about this. There was a time that I was very angry with her for telling my mother that the abuser did not stain my dress. You may ask why I never spoke with my cousin about the situation. At the time, I feared she would probably deny what she said. More importantly, as I got older, it became difficult to face the fact that my mom did not believe me. My mom did not investigate what was on my dress, nor did she ever ask me about what really happened. I wondered what she actually thought was on my dress. What was on her mind when she washed the dress? Did she examine it or just throw it in the washing machine? I will never know because there was no other discussion about what happened to me that day. Although my mom and cousin moved on with their day, no one knew how deeply it affected me. The abuser was able to continue what he was doing to me because no one ever addressed it. Perhaps, if they had believed me and intervened, it would have stopped.

I am not sure how many times I was violated; however, I know it happened several times. When I visited my best friend to play, the perpetrator would force me to do things that I didn't want to do. He even attempted to penetrate me, but his penis was too large. However, this did not stop him. He said things to convince me that it was okay. He said he loved me and was going to marry me. A girl's dream! My dream was to marry the one I love. He persuaded my immature mind to think that it was okay because he was going to marry me. Wow! How manipulative to play on the emotions of a child. I have come to understand through God's Word that the perpetrator was a thief who used the word *love* to manipulate and control me. In John 10:10, it states that "the thief comes to steal, kill and destroy." The perpetrator stole my innocence and twisted all those ideas and imageries that I had as a young girl about what it meant to be husband and wife.

REFLECTION

When parents and other adults have the opportunity to intervene on behalf of a child who has been abused, may they have the courage to confront the evil that has infiltrated their lives.

~ *Reflections* ~
Write Your Thoughts

SIX
Daddy, Am I?

I am happy to say that the sexual abuse did stop. However, I can't pinpoint exactly when. I have a clear memory of what the perpetrator did to me. It's interesting how the mind remembers. What is more profound, is how the mind attempts to handle something so traumatic. It remembers and tries to deal with the suffering and pain that shows up in our everyday lives. I have always been crazy about boys. As I said earlier, I played with dolls and dreamt of being married. It may have been a fairytale thought; however, it was my story. Satan, who is the killer of dreams, attempted to snatch this away from me.

You may be asking, "How could it be snatched away?" The Bible tells us that the devil comes to steal, kill and destroy. I am more aware of his schemes now than I have ever been in my entire life. I was very vulnerable to the devil's attacks when I was young. As I was maturing, the abuse caused me to suffer a blow to my sexual development. Erikson's Stage 5 (Adolescence), addresses such situations. The conflict to be resolved is "Identity vs. Role Confusion." He explains, "The teenager must achieve a sense of identity in occupation, sex roles, politics, and religion." I questioned myself with, "Who am I?" "Do I love boys as I used to?" "Do I like girls?" "Who am I?"

Sexual identity is defined as "How one thinks of oneself in terms of to whom one is romantically or sexually attracted" (Wikipedia contributors, "Sexual Identity," n.d.). What my pastor told me when I was young had farther-reaching effects than he could have ever possibly anticipated. He told me that if I had sex one time, I would know if I was gay. This will be further addressed in the following pages. Who we are attracted to is only one dimension of who we are. It is not the whole of

27

who we are. I was in crisis. I stayed in a state of rejection. I rejected myself and suffered from self-loathing and self-condemnation.

I did not understand what it meant to be gay. The thought was introduced one day when I was watching the TV show, *Alice*. Alice was a widow who had one son and worked at a diner. In this episode, she went on a date, after a long period of being alone. After a wonderful evening, I recall Alice's date surprising her by saying that he was gay. That was the first time I had ever heard this word. I will never forget the look on Alice's face, and her saying something to the effect of "So, you don't like women." After hearing the guy say that he was gay, the thought became haunting. It tormented me, and I could not shake it. I tried to get the thought out of my mind, but I couldn't. Whatever it meant to be gay, I wanted nothing to do with it.

I went to my father when I was about eleven or twelve years old and asked him, "Am I gay?" My dad told me to get that thought out of my head and not think about it again. Once again, I tried to get the thought out of my head; however, it would not leave. I decided to go to my pastor and ask him if I was gay. So one day after church, I waited until he was by himself and asked. The pastor went to the Bible and pointed his finger to a section that talked about an animal. He began to tell me that this is what women were and I scoffed. I was standing behind him, looking over his shoulder, as he sat at his desk. Since I was not getting the answer that I was looking for, I asked him if I had to have sex to know if I was gay or straight. It was then that he turned around, looked me in the eyes, and said, "If you have sex one time, then you will know if you are gay or straight." I left his office satisfied with his response but terrified at the same time. It seemed logical to me that if I did what he said, then I would no longer be confused about who I was. Sadly, the two men in my life, whom I trusted most: my dad and my pastor, were not able to answer the question.

28

How many of you know that "Am I gay?" was *not* the real question? The real question was simply, "Who am I?" The thought of "Who am I?" was accompanied by betrayal and rejection, which were engraved upon my mind.

I know that homosexuality is now more acceptable in our society. My heart goes out to those who have struggled with sexual identity. This is a real struggle, and it is tormenting. The Bible says in 1 Corinthians 6:16 that when sexual sin is committed, the two become one flesh. A child cannot understand that he or she has become one with the sexual abuser. He or she has then been placed in a position of vulnerability and cannot understand their mental, physical, emotional and spiritual state. Children's inability to properly process the sexual abuse can lead many to a life of distortion.

God, Save Me ...

My torment and confusion led to superstitious, obsessive, and perfectionistic behaviors. For instance, not stepping on sidewalk cracks meant I wasn't gay. Avoiding television programs that dealt with sexuality kept me from feeling overwhelmed. Of course, participating in sex with a male told me that I wasn't gay. I continually repeated these behaviors, so I wouldn't believe the thoughts that were tormenting me. I felt drained and depleted.

I begged God to take the behaviors away. I tried to understand the Word of God, but when I read it, it just seemed to say that God was angry and would kill massive numbers of people. I so desperately wanted God's love and yet, it seemed so far off. When I sang, I felt close to God, and I loved being in the presence of God's people. Drawn to God and His church, I also drew strength in the midst of my confusion.

I continued this life of promiscuity throughout my early adulthood. I wanted so badly to be accepted for who I was, but I didn't know who I was. I needed that question answered. I needed to know that an ugly and despicable act had been committed against me, but it was not my fault. I needed to know that I was loved, and yes, I was who God said I was. Sex never helped me to determine who I was; it only served to confuse me more. Males were placed in charge of healing my greatest hurts. Isn't this what people do? We expect others to nurture us and give meaning to our lives. That is too much pressure for any one person to handle. Often, the people that we desire to heal us are broken themselves.

As I was growing up, my dad used to tell me about the importance of not engaging in sex with different men. He would say, "Regina, don't be a revolving door." I didn't understand what my dad meant at the time, but as I continued to engage in sex, it became clear. He wanted me to treat my body with dignity and respect. There was such guilt, shame, and condemnation after the act. I also struggled with the fact that I had become that revolving door.

I did not start healing from these tragic circumstances until after I was married and had a strong desire to be a better wife. I wanted to be married because I desired to please God, by living my life as He intended. I was having sex outside of marriage and felt that I would go to hell if I continued. 1 Samuel 16:7 states,

> But the Lord said to Samuel, 'Do not consider his appearance or his height, for I have rejected him. The Lord does not look at the things people look at. People look at the outward appearance, but the Lord looks at the heart.'

Let's take a deeper look at this verse. It states that the Lord looks at the heart.

The Lord knew my heart was full of turmoil. He also knew that I was living a tormented life. When I say "a tormented life," I am mostly speaking of the mental anguish, which was the aftermath of the sexual abuse. I had no idea of the amount of pain I carried. My life was full of fear, anxiety and loneliness. I felt that the remedy to my anguish would be for me to get married. Boy, was I wrong! Proverbs 14:12 states, "There is a way which seemeth right unto a man, but the end thereof are the ways of death" (King James Version). I was locked in my own understanding. I wanted to be loved, admired and respected. Most importantly, I wanted God's love.

REFLECTION

God knows everything about us, and He would not reject us as His children. He wants to heal us and get involved in what's troubling, tormenting and bringing turmoil into our lives. God knows His plans for us and desires for us to live them out.

'For I know the plans I have for you,' declares the Lord, 'plans to prosper you and not to harm you, plans to give you hope and a future. Then you will call on me and come and pray to me, and I will listen to you. You will seek me and find me when you seek me with all your heart.' (Jeremiah 29:11-13)

~ *Reflections* ~
Write Your Thoughts

SEVEN
Realizations

1 Corinthians 13:11-12

[11] When I was a child, I talked like a child, I thought like a child, I reasoned like a child. When I became a man, I put the ways of childhood behind me. [12] For now we see only a reflection as in a mirror; then we shall see face to face. Now I know in part; then I shall know fully, even as I am fully known.

1 Corinthians 13:11 tells us about childlike behavior. I love this Scripture. As a mother and once a child myself, I now see through the eyes of my daughter, the childlike behavior I once had. When I reflect on going through that door and my mother asking me what was on my dress, I hear my childlike response. I said the person's name. My cousin immediately responded, "Aunt Essie, I don't believe that." I was too young to understand whatever adult thoughts were on my cousin's mind. It is imperative for parents to understand what it means to have childlike behavior. My parents' failure to investigate what happened started me on a journey of constantly questioning myself about whether or not I was telling the truth. I would hear the thoughts in my mind saying "You're lying." I started living a life of checking and rechecking. I also found myself needlessly apologizing for things I was not doing. I lived a life of self-doubt and false guilt.

When I consider "Eric Erickson's 8 Stages of Psychosocial Development," I realize my experiences occurred during stages 4 and 5, "Latency and Adolescence" (Erikson 2017). This is depicted in the chart on the next pages:

Stage	Ages	Basic Conflict	Important Event	Summary
1. Oral-Sensory	12 to 18 months		Feeding	The infant must form a first loving, trusting relationship with the caregiver, or develop a sense of mistrust.
2. Muscular-Anal	18 months to 3 years	Autonomy vs. Shame/ Doubt	Toilet training	The child's energies are directed toward the development of physical skills, including walking, grasping, and rectal sphincter control. The child learns control but may develop shame and doubt if not handled well.
3. Loco-motor	3 to 6 years	Initiative vs Guilt	Independ-ence	The child continues to become more assertive and to take more initiative but may be too forceful, leading to guilt feelings.

Stage	Ages	Basic Conflict	Important Event	Summary
4. Latency	6 to 12 years	Industry vs Inferiority	School	The child must deal with demands to learn new skills or risk a sense of inferiority, failure, and incompetence.
5. Adoles-cence	12 to 18 years	Identity vs. Role Confusion	Peer relation-ships	The teenager must achieve a sense of identity in occupation, sex roles, politics, and religion.
6. Young Adult	19 to 40 years	Intimacy vs isolation	Love relation-ships	The young adult must develop intimate relationships or suffer feelings of isolation.
7. Middle Adult-hood	40 to 65 years	Generativity vs Stagnation	Parenting	Each adult must find some way to satisfy and support the next generation.
8. Maturity	65 to death	Ego Integrity vs Despair	Reflection on and acceptance of one's life	The culmination is a sense of oneself as one is and of feeling fulfilled.

35

In Erikson's Stage 4 – Industry vs. Inferiority, it states that "The child must deal with demands to learn new skills or risk a sense of inferiority, failure, and incompetence." I was often angry and defensive. I constantly fought with my siblings and stayed in trouble during my elementary, junior high, and some of my high school years. I dealt with rejection, fear, abandonment, and acceptance. I felt that I was not good enough and I often wondered if I would find a true friend.

Although it was rough, I also had things in my life that brought salvation. The church choir and glee club at school were my hiding places. I also enjoyed running. I learned how to sew, crochet, and knit. It was my father who taught me how to crochet and knit. In middle school, I knitted a vest for my big white and green stuffed rabbit that my cousin and his fiancé purchased for me. I sewed a pretty blue jean outfit that was showcased at my middle school. My sewing teacher, Ms. Edwards, saw all of her students as beautiful. She would say that there were no ugly children. Mrs. Edwards made me feel like I was the most beautiful person in the world.

My involvement in extracurricular activities continued throughout high school. High school was tough. I did not have the best relationships with some of my teachers, and I was getting into trouble. However, I wanted to turn things around. Some of the kids that I grew up with were excelling, and I didn't want to be left behind. God placed another "Ms. Edwards" into my life. Her name was Ms. Robinson. She was my typing teacher, and I loved her. She made me feel accepted. She spent extra time teaching me how to type. I enjoyed typing and being with her. She helped me to believe in myself. I also joined the track team. Again, God placed another gentle person in my life; this time it was Coach Scott. My geometry teacher, Mr. Carnegie, also blessed my life.

There was a small group of girls that I had known since elementary school. I repeatedly set myself up for rejection because I wanted to join them. I constantly asked if could hang out with them, only to hear a resounding "No." However, around the 11th grade, the friend group parted ways. I was able to build a friendship with one of the girls, and it had a great impact on my life. Her friendship meant a great deal to me, and we spent a lot of time together. We often caught the bus from school to downtown Detroit and ate at McDonald's. We talked for hours on the telephone. It was special having her in my life. I had other friends who would visit and sleep over at times. I started to study harder, staying up day and night, striving to improve my grades. I wanted to be an honor student and be seen in a different light by teachers and peers. As a result of making these changes, life became a little easier.

REFLECTION

Lord, bless those who have suffered trauma with caring and loving adults. Provide activities and experiences for them that bring hope and encouragement. Bless them with a circle of friends and peers that promote acceptance.

~ *Reflections* ~
Write Your Thoughts

EIGHT
Daddy, Console Me

One summer day I was sitting on my porch enjoying the sun. All of a sudden there was the abuser, talking to me from his mother's porch. Our houses sat adjacent to each other. I am not sure about the conversation, but I believe he wanted me to come closer to him. I did not want to, so I refused to leave my porch. I was in my teens by then.

My dad came out of the house and saw us talking. When the abuser saw my dad, he spoke to him, and he moved on. My dad didn't say anything else to me. Later that evening I was in our basement, and my dad approached me. He said that the abuser could not have had sex with me because I was still talking to him. I was shocked that he said those words to me. I had no idea, up until that moment, that he knew what the abuser had done. I never told him what happened. I started to wonder, "Am I supposed to be angry with him?" This was the first time that I realized how I should act toward the abuser. Throughout my teen years, I was concerned about being around him. I didn't understand all the ramifications of what he had done, but I knew he had wronged me. What was most surprising was to hear my dad say that I had sex with him. I recall thinking, "Sex? I had sex with him?" I was truly clueless about what feelings I should have had. I stood in the presence of my dad, once again having to defend myself.

As I grew older, I saw less and less of the perpetrator. I would see him with his female friends, and he seemed to spend less time at his mother's home. Seeing that he had female friends was hurtful because he told me that he was going to marry me. I felt so betrayed. How could he have other girls? It was difficult dealing with the realities of what he did to me, along with the fact that he had no intention of following through with what he promised.

These feelings may seem odd to you. You may be saying, "He abused you. How could you want to be with him?" I think a helpful way to look at this is through the eyes of David's daughter Tamar, whose story is found in 2 Samuel 13:1-22.

[1] In the course of time, Amnon son of David fell in love with Tamar, the beautiful sister of Absalom son of David.

[2] Amnon became so obsessed with his sister Tamar that he made himself ill. She was a virgin, and it seemed impossible for him to do anything to her.

[3] Now Amnon had an adviser named Jonadab son of Shimeah, David's brother. Jonadab was a very shrewd man.

[4] He asked Amnon, "Why do you, the king's son, look so haggard morning after morning? Won't you tell me?" Amnon said to him, "I'm in love with Tamar, my brother Absalom's sister."

[5] "Go to bed and pretend to be ill," Jonadab said. "When your father comes to see you, say to him, 'I would like my sister Tamar to come and give me something to eat. Let her prepare the food in my sight so I may watch her and then eat it from her hand.'

[6] So Amnon lay down and pretended to be ill. When the king came to see him, Amnon said to him, "I would like my sister Tamar to come and make some special bread in my sight, so I may eat from her hand."

[7] David sent word to Tamar at the palace: "Go to the house of your brother Amnon and prepare some food for him."

[8] So Tamar went to the house of her brother Amnon, who was lying down. She took some dough, kneaded it, made the bread in his sight and baked it.

[9] Then she took the pan and served him the bread, but he refused to eat. "Send everyone out of here," Amnon said. So everyone left him.

[10] Then Amnon said to Tamar, "Bring the food here into my bedroom so I may eat from your hand." And Tamar took the

bread she had prepared and brought it to her brother Amnon in his bedroom. [11] But when she took it to him to eat, he grabbed her and said, "Come to bed with me, my sister." [12] "No, my brother!" she said to him. Don't force me! Such a thing should not be done in Israel! Don't do this wicked thing. [13] What about me? Where could I get rid of my disgrace? And what about you? You would be like one of the wicked fools in Israel. Please speak to the king; he will not keep me from being married to you." [14] But he refused to listen to her, and since he was stronger than she, he raped her.

[15] Then Amnon hated her with intense hatred. In fact, he hated her more than he had loved her. Amnon said to her, "Get up and get out!" [16] "No!" she said to him. "Sending me away would be a greater wrong than what you have already done to me." But he refused to listen to her.

[17] He called his personal servant and said, "Get this woman out of my sight and bolt the door after her." [18] So his servant put her out and bolted the door after her. She was wearing an ornate robe, for this was the kind of garment the virgin daughters of the king wore. [19] Tamar put ashes on her head and tore the ornate robe she was wearing. She put her hands on her head and went away, weeping aloud as she went.

[20] Her brother Absalom said to her, "Has that Amnon, your brother, been with you? Be quiet for now, my sister; he is your brother. Don't take this thing to heart." And Tamar lived in her brother Absalom's house, a desolate woman. [21] When King David heard all this, he was furious. [22] And Absalom never said a word to Amnon, either good or bad; he hated Amnon because he had disgraced his sister Tamar.

When reading about Tamar, you get a sense of her identity. Tamar lived in the palace with her father, King David. You also learn that Amnon was her half-brother, but she and Absalom had the same mother and father. However, her mother is mentioned only once in Scripture. Tamar followed the customs of Israelite women. She wore an ornate robe, signifying that she was a virgin. As I write about Tamar, I desire to honor her voice. One of the ways I choose to honor her is by acknowledging her story and shedding light on her experience. Another way of honoring her voice is by recognizing that she suffered in silence. I intend to give voice and a sense of hope to those who suffer in silence, by saying to them, "You are not alone."

When I read about what Amnon did to his sister, it was heartbreaking. The story of what happened to Tamar has all the elements of how rape is commonly perceived. Tamar was caught off-guard, coerced, and fully aware of what her abuser was doing to her. Tamar desperately tried to reason with and convince him not to commit this heinous crime against her. However, her voice fell on deaf ears. Clearly, for Amnon, it was about power, control and taking what he wanted without considering the cost.

Although our experiences differ, I can relate to Tamar's emotions. Her brother was her abuser, and mine was my next-door neighbor. Tamar was a young woman who was saving herself for her husband. She took pride and joy in following the laws and expectations of her culture. I would have to say that in my heart and mind, I was doing the same. She was saving herself for her husband, and it was shown outwardly by the garment that she wore. As a child, I dreamt of my wedding gown being white, as my dad walked me down the aisle to present me to my husband. In our culture, the white gown represented purity.

I realize that we live in a society that no longer values the tradition of a woman "saving herself" for her spouse. When I was growing up, marriage was valued, and the culture demonstrated such. I once read that you can see the trend of society by observing what is shown on television. Just look at our culture today, and you will see it displayed on the screen.

There is a need for me to address Tamar's well-being. This tragedy left a permanent footprint, and it was irreversible. Tamar was robbed of her innocence. The Bible tells us that she enjoyed a sense of freedom and security. She enjoyed the luxuries of life that most girls were unable to experience, and she wore it proudly. Tamar embraced her cultural beliefs, and this is why she pleaded with Amnon. Look at 2 Samuel 13:12-16 again:

[12] "No, my brother!" she said to him. Don't force me! Such a thing should not be done in Israel! Don't do this wicked thing.
[13] What about me? Where could I get rid of my disgrace? And what about you? You would be like one of the wicked fools in Israel. Please speak to the king; he will not keep me from being married to you."
[14] But he refused to listen to her, and since he was stronger than she, he raped her.
[15] Then Amnon hated her with intense hatred. In fact he hated her more than he had loved her. Amnon said to her, "Get up and get out!"
[16] "No!" she said to him. "Sending me away would be a greater wrong than what you have already done to me."

When Tamar walked into her brother's room, she rendered an act of kindness toward him, but he rendered an act of violence and saddled her with disgrace and shame. After he raped her, she tore her garment in half and placed ashes on her forehead. The ashes signified mourning. Tamar tells us that the rape was against Israel, and also against God. She knew that if Amnon committed this crime, it was going to impact more than just herself. Israel would be defiled. Leviticus 18:9 (KJV) reads, "The nakedness of thy sister, the daughter of thy father, or daughter of thy mother, whether she be born at home, or born abroad, even their nakedness thou shalt not uncover."

Amnon knew that he was forbidden to uncover his sister's nakedness. He was knowledgeable of the laws of Israel and how important it was for a woman to remain a virgin until marriage. She lost everything that day. Her hopes were dashed and her dreams of marriage destroyed. The course of her life was rewritten. Amnon stripped her of her dignity, pride, and purity. She was betrayed.

Why Me?

As difficult as this story is to digest, it demonstrates to us that rape and molestation have been a part of the world for over 2000 years. Sadly, it will continue to be so. You may ask how a loving God could allow something so tragic to occur. I have asked that same question. The simplest answer God gave me was that we live in a dark and evil world, and destructive acts happen. You see, I have learned that when you put the responsibility for the act on the person who did it, then you deal with the behavior of that person. Yes, God could have stopped the act from happening. However, God also grants us free will. We have the power to choose right from wrong. If God doesn't stop tragedy from occurring, then we tend to question what type of God He is. God is not always going to prevent us from experiencing hardship. However, He will bring us through every circumstance because He is a loving God (Isaiah 43:2).

God had promised that King David's family would suffer division (2 Samuel 12:7-12). The hideous act that Amnon committed against Tamar might have been just one of the events that caused division and calamity. I find this to be a sensible process of elimination, due to the sinful act he committed against Bathsheba's husband, Uriah (2 Samuel 11:1-16). Often, we can't figure out why certain things transpire. We can speculate, but we really don't know the reason why things happen. It is a question that is often asked by a victim: "Why did this happen to me?" I know that at one point, I asked that same plaguing question: "Why?" I was able to find comfort in Romans 8:28. "And we know that in all things God works for the good of those who love him, who have been called according to His purpose."

Tamar's life speaks to the significant impact that rape can have on one's ability to keep living. Her story also demonstrates what can happen if appropriate measures to deal with the transgression are not taken. 2 Samuel 13:20 states, "Her brother Absalom said to her, 'Has that Amnon, your brother, been with you? Be quiet for now, my sister; he is your brother. Don't take this thing to heart.'" From that point on, Tamar lived in Absalom's house as "a desolate woman." His terrible advice silenced her. This is similar to how I was silenced by those in my life who refused to believe that I had been abused.

Desolate is defined as "barren or laid waste; devastated." (Dictionary.com, n.d., "Desolate"). The Bible tells us that Absalom instructed Tamar not to take this to heart and to be quiet, "that is your brother." Just as rape is permeated throughout the earth, so is such advice. Surviving sexual assault has taught me that many people may treat the act with disregard. How could Tamar *not* take it to heart? Victims are often left to deal with the aftermath alone. As a counselor, I have come across a few families that have responded with sincere assurance to the victims and also sought to get help for the perpetrators.

We don't hear the voice of Tamar's mother. This was not unusual in the Bible. Again, referring to the culture of that time, it is understood that women's voices were rarely heard. The Scripture notes in 2 Samuel 13:21-22 (KJV):

²¹ But when King David heard of all these things, he was very angry.
²²And Absalom spoke to his brother Amnon neither good nor bad. For Absalom hated Amnon, because he had forced his sister Tamar.

The Bible does not give any indication that David spoke with Amnon about the sexual assault. It does not share that David comforted his daughter Tamar. However, we do see that David was furious with Amnon. Unfortunately, not furious enough to confront his son nor console his daughter. I also dealt with my parents' lack of response in securing my emotional well-being. I believe the Word of God does an exceptional job demonstrating human responses to life experiences.

Why didn't David punish Amnon for his sin against Tamar? One source states,

> Many reasons have been suggested. One likely reason is that Amnon was David's son and that David had been guilty of sexual sin himself (in the case of Bathsheba)—therefore, in the case of Amnon and Tamar, he felt inadequate to judge. Another possible reason is that there was no witness to the crime. Amnon's friend Jonadab had carefully orchestrated the crime to avoid the possibility of witnesses; therefore, there was no way to prove the crime according to Jewish law. (Got Questions, n.d.)

Regardless of the reason, Absalom took matters into his own hands. He avenged Tamar by killing their half-brother. The murder caused many problems for his family. Absalom was isolated from his family for three years to save his life. He lived for an additional period in Jerusalem before seeing his father's face again. Sadly, Absalom would later seek to usurp his father's throne, resulting in his own death.

The Bible tells us that his father deeply grieved for him. Absalom and Tamar's lives had tragic endings. Her story reveals that rape has heartbreaking consequences.

Twisted Lies

Throughout my teen years, I struggled with having feelings for the man who abused me. My dating years were filled with conflict. He had always said that he was going to marry me, and yet I saw others. My parents allowed me to have male visitors at age sixteen, but I was not allowed to go places with them. I had to be seventeen years old to go on an actual date. I was constantly vulnerable during these visits because I didn't know how to engage with boys properly.

One day I was walking to the store near my home. I am not sure where the abuser came from, but I saw him coming toward me. That entire day I had sensed a heaviness on me, like doom. The day seemed dark, and I couldn't shake the heavy feeling. I felt that something was going to happen to me. As the abuser came closer, he walked with anger and deliberateness. While this was happening, his girlfriend was sitting on his mother's porch, urgently calling his name as he continued to walk toward me. I tried to switch gears and head back to my house. When he approached me, she was then standing up screaming his name. I could feel in the air that he was going to do something to me. I was stricken with fear.

He pinned me against a brick wall and was visibly angry, saying, "I bet' not see you with anyone!" I tried standing my ground telling him to get away from me and that he had a girlfriend. This moment was very intense and overwhelming for me. He finally let me go and started walking back toward the woman. I decided to go back in the direction of the store because I wasn't sure what he or the woman would try to do to me.

I eventually went home but was fearful. However, that day I vowed that he wasn't going to control who I dated. I didn't want him to see who I was dating, but I also wasn't going to allow him to dictate my life. Mustering up the strength to ward him off worked to my advantage. Subsequently, there was another encounter with him, but I had the strength to emphatically tell him that I was going to see whomever I wanted.

REFLECTION

Lord, bless those who have had similar experiences as Tamar and I. Thank you for the family members who get involved, experience the pain, and desire to protect the abused. Please give moms, dads, and families the knowledge, insight, and response that brings forth healing.

~ *Reflections* ~
Write Your Thoughts

NINE
An Undivided Heart

Parasitical Love

Ezekiel 11:19-20 reads,

I will give them an undivided heart and put a new spirit in them; I will remove from them their heart of stone and give them a heart of flesh. Then they will follow my decrees and be careful to keep my laws. They will be my people, and I will be their God.

This Scripture, like many others, transformed my life. When I started my healing process, I prayed that God would heal the brokenness of my heart. I was in my early 30s. I was married, wanted to be a good wife, and had finally found a safe place. My husband and I were excited to be with each other. There was no one else for us. We were living and breathing one another from the beginning of our relationship. We didn't want anyone to tell us we could not be together. The relationship was parasitical. *Parasitic* is mainly a scientific term for "an organism that lives on a host, taking what it needs to stay alive while often injuring the host" (Vocabulary.com, n.d., "Parasitic").

I recall the first time that my fiancé took me to meet his mother. I was looking forward to meeting someone who was very motherly and loving. I imagined a mother-in-law who would love me. I had visions of us being best friends and enjoying much laughter. Instead, I met a very poor version of this vision—not only physically but spiritually. It was clear during my first encounter with her that this woman worked to drain the life out of her son. My fiancé was excited for his mother to meet me, but the greeting he received shattered his spirit and made me feel uncomfortable. When I met her, I walked into a home that was not very presentable and encountered a woman who was angry. Our first meeting did not go well, and unfortunately, it set the tone for the rest of our relationship.

I had a similar experience with my brother when I took my fiancé to meet him and his family. My fiancé and I were very touchy with each other. If we were watching television, we watched from the same chair. We were always hugging, kissing, and in one another's presence. I understood that my brother didn't want his children exposed to our public displays of affection, so I attempted to respect that. Moreover, I understood that we couldn't sleep in the same room with each other, but it was difficult to stop being affectionate with him. My brother and I got into it, so my fiance and I decided to get a room. The attitude that prevailed in our relationship was that no one was going to get in the way of us being together. We were in love.

Reaching for Real Love

I had committed to the Lord that if He allowed me to marry, I would dedicate my life to Him. I was already saved and desired to live a sanctified life. I had heard myself, and other women say, "I just want to be married. I feel so alone." We believed that marriage would resolve our heartaches. However, the Scripture says, "I will give them an undivided heart." Wow, this is powerful. A woman seeks what she believes will bring life because her heart is often divided. What does it mean to have a divided heart? Well, read my story:

My husband at the time was supportive, gentle, encouraging, and full of laughter. We found a nice townhouse and, for the most part, we thought we were happy. There were times I did not feel clean in my marriage. I often thought of the song lyrics, "Lord give me a clean heart, and I will follow you."

My mind was fighting all types of battles, and I had overwhelming fear. These struggles were happening all in the midst of feeling good about the man I had married. Furthermore, by this time, I had started taking classes at seminary. I knew that God had a call on my life.

Remember what I said earlier? I made a promise to God that if He allowed me to marry, I would dedicate my life to Him. So, in my efforts to keep my promise to God, I started seeking His face by reading His Word daily. I desperately wanted peace and had been using external methods. Only God could lead me down the path of healing and wholeness. I now realize that God had already started me on that journey. I will explain that later on.

It is so true that only God can heal a broken heart. I was broken and in need of a heart transplant. I thought that since I was married, I would no longer be conflicted about sex. However, I didn't know how to be a wife, friend, or lover. I thought my love for him would be enough for us to survive. How little did I really know? I recall televangelist Joyce Meyer saying "Hurting people hurt people." My, how this resonated with me. I came to understand that what I brought to my marriage were broken pieces and a divided heart. Unfortunately, my husband brought the same.

The more I read God's Word, it seemed the more unstable I became. I began experiencing flashbacks of the abuse and intrusive thoughts. I started to lose a lot of weight, have high and low mood swings and poor sleep. I was tearful and afraid, could not eat, and heard voices. I also had suicidal and homicidal thoughts. I was an emotional wreck. I cried daily, and my husband did not know how to help. I found myself talking back to the voices in my head, and this was scary. I became anxious and would go to a corner of my living room and cry out to God, day and night. I stayed in God's Word and His presence, even though the thoughts and flashbacks became more aggressive.

A friend said that it was as if I was drowning in a pot of water. The same friend became my prayer partner. I was blessed to have her as my prayer partner, and we prayed every Monday. Of course, I leaned on her more as my situation intensified. She recommended that I see a psychiatrist to be evaluated for medication. I couldn't disagree. I was mentally drained and in a real battle for my sanity. Furthermore, as a medical professional, I feared that her recommendation could have been cause for psychiatric hospitalization. I could have been perceived as a danger to myself and others.

Thankfully, I had drawn near to God and could hear His voice. It amazed me how I was able to hear the voice of God through all the mental anguish. The Lord spoke to me and told me that I did not need medications and that He was my Healer. When I told my prayer partner that God said I didn't need meds, she did not say a word. She just stayed in the battle with me. However, she was probably contemplating whether or not I actually heard from God.

My husband was a safe place for me in the early part of our marriage. I know this is why I was able to start the healing process. As I previously stated, I drew closer to God by reading His Word. In our bedroom, I would read for hours at a time. It was very therapeutic. I could not stop hungering for God. The Word says, "Come near to God, and He will come near to you" (James 4:8). God drew near to me. Boy, was I in for a makeover! When we choose to draw near to God, He will reciprocate. God will do a new thing in you. "Forget the former things and do not dwell on the past. See, I am doing a new thing! Now it springs up; do you perceive it?" (Isaiah 43:18). I could not perceive what God was going to do in me. The only thing I knew, was that I was in great pain. It was as if God had taken a gigantic Band-Aid off my heart, exposed my open wound and literally left me to die.

I knew I needed counseling. It was refreshing to know a pastor like Dr. Frederick G. Sampson of Tabernacle Missionary Baptist Church in Detroit. I felt like one of his daughters and had a great opportunity to grow in the Word of God under his leadership. I met with Dr. Sampson several times, and he gave great advice and guidance. Although he was a sincere, spiritual and powerful pastor, I sensed that something more was needed. I eventually sought help elsewhere, while I continued to seek his help for my spiritual development.

Another girlfriend of mine was participating in evening programs that Mt. Zion Church in Clarkston, Michigan offered for healing and restoration. She enjoyed the classes and felt that I would also benefit. I was a little skeptical, but felt that I had nothing to lose. A sense of peace engulfed me as I walked through the doors of the Church. I immediately knew that I was in the right place. I attended weekly classes and even sought counseling sessions. My counselor helped me to understand that I was on God's operating table and she was there to help guide me.

During the time I attended Mt. Zion, I listened to daily radio programs such as Dr. Charles Stanley, Joyce Meyers and June Hunt. As I stayed in the process, I experienced deliverance, restoration, peace, and newness of life. I am forever grateful for every prayer warrior at the altar who poured life-changing words into my hearing. The fellowship and love of others helped me to see that I was not alone. It became clear that there were hurting people in the world. Mt. Zion made it a part of their mission to participate in God setting the captives free (Isaiah 61:1-3).

Ezekiel 11 spoke to me about having a divided heart, which displeased God. He truly wants us to be sold out to Him and trust Him as master over our lives. Many Scriptures warn against being lukewarm and tossed to and fro by any wind of doctrine. By suffering the blow of sexual abuse, emotional, mental, sexual, and spiritual divisions were created in my heart. God wasn't trying to destroy me when He uncovered my wound. He was actually healing me, to become a woman of sound mind, heart, and soul.

REFLECTION

Lord, I pray for those who have divided hearts, and are tormented and unable to see a way out. I pray, Dear God, that You will lead them on paths of righteousness for Your Name's sake. As your daughters seek a clear path, let them also discern when others might try to take advantage and cause more harm.

~ *Reflections* ~
Write Your Thoughts

TEN
Forgiveness

Hatred stirs up conflict, but love covers over all wrongs (Proverbs 10:12).

I was so angry with God because I felt He expected too much from me. Nevertheless, I loved Him. What a paradox! In my eyes, God was my condemner. He was distant and displeased with me. I strived to be perfect and was methodical in my behavior. This was a stressful life to live. As much as I saw God as my condemner, I could not live without Him. Deep down in my soul, I knew He loved me.

Later on, I learned that my views of God were distorted and misguided. One day while in a seminary class, I was experiencing the tormenting thoughts again and I audibly responded to them. I was striving to be discreet and didn't want to be embarrassed or laughed at, but it was overpowering. I fought back against the thoughts with my words. However, they would not go away. I looked around to see if anyone could see me and two classmates were laughing. I wanted to disappear within myself. The harder I tried to focus on the instructor it seemed the louder the thoughts.

After class was over, I tried to dash to my car. One of my classmates, Rev. Jimmie D. Compton, Jr., introduced himself and inquired about my relationship with God. I shared my thoughts about God and His expectations of me. Right away, he knew that I had a lot of Scriptures in me, but I was missing the foundational of truths of the Bible. He invited me to a class that he taught at his Church, on the foundational teachings of understanding God. We met for about six weeks. His teaching changed my life. No longer did I see God as a distant condemner who expected too much of me. I then saw God as my friend and empathizer. He loved me and cared about everything that I was experiencing. I was no longer angry with God, and He was not disappointed with me. I was and am forgiven.

I have learned that what doesn't make sense to us makes perfect sense to God. The Word tells us in Proverbs 3:5-6

> Trust in the Lord with all your heart, And lean not on your own understanding; In all your ways acknowledge Him, And He shall direct your paths. (New King James Version)

One day my prayer partner and I were on the phone, and as we were praying, she said that the Lord was instructing me to apologize to my mom. I kind of chuckled and got an attitude with God. She ministered to me and encouraged me to follow as God instructed. As encouraging as she was, she only sounded like Charlie Brown's teacher: "wonk, wonk, wonk, wonk, wonk." I determined in my heart that I was not going to follow through with an apology.

The Lord sent another messenger, and this time it was my hair stylist. As she was styling my hair on this particular day, the Lord told her that I needed to apologize to my mom. I couldn't believe that now my hair stylist was saying this to me. I turned my head toward her and asked in disbelief, "What did you say?" She repeated that the Lord told her that I needed to apologize to my mom. I thought to myself, "Why is the Lord telling me to do this?" This was exhausting for me! He knew that she was the one who wronged me; not the other way around. My hair stylist also ministered to me and I decided that day I needed to follow God's instructions. As I accepted the fact that I would apologize to Mom, I started to think that maybe she would apologize too.

I finally apologized to my mom for my disrespect, disobedience and smart mouth toward her. Although I did as the Lord instructed, my Mom did not apologize for the way she had treated me. I walked away feeling betrayed and stuck. God had to teach me a couple of additional lessons in this area of forgiveness before I got it. One day I was driving in my vehicle and fussing in my spirit about my mom not apologizing. I felt led to listen to a radio program and heard a woman teaching God's Word. She referenced Romans 12:3.

For I say, through the grace given to me, to everyone who is among you, not to think of himself more highly than he ought to think, but to think soberly, as God has dealt to each one a measure of faith. (NKJV)

The words "do not think more highly of yourself than you ought to" strongly resonated in my spirit. I began to reflect on the verse. As the speaker continued to teach, the Lord spoke and said, "You think too highly of yourself." Well, this couldn't be the case, because as far as I was concerned, my self-esteem was at the bottom of my shoe.

Immediately, the Lord brought revelation about this word. He showed me that I indeed thought too highly of myself. The lesson that I learned was that regardless of how my mom treated me, I needed to honor her as my mother.

"Honor your father and your mother …" (Exodus 20:12). I know that for some people the words "honor your mother" may not resonate and may sound insulting. I am not suggesting that anyone stay in an abusive relationship. Honoring your mother and father could simply mean respecting them for the title of parent. The Lord showed me that I didn't think much of my mother. My mom was the woman whom God had chosen to guide me into the woman I would become. I can honestly say now, in my older years, that I am my mother's daughter. The woman I rejected, I have now become.

I continued to listen to Christian radio as I healed. In a certain broadcast, a young lady spoke about forgiveness. She explained that asking others for forgiveness doesn't mean that they will also admit what they have done. Wow, this was deep. I couldn't believe my ears. What kind of forgiveness was that?

It seemed one-sided, but I still got the message. This message of forgiveness was intended for me. It was not for my mom. God was interested in healing me. God was doing a new thing in me, and I needed to receive it and not worry about my mom. It was then clear to me that forgiveness is for the person who has been wronged or hurt. Extending forgiveness is not for the other person. Forgiveness is internal and brings healing to the bones. It is not external and meant to change the other person. This was extremely difficult to do, and I failed at times. Nevertheless, I knew that God saw me as a work in progress.

One day, I was driving my mom somewhere, and I spoke with her about my hurts. The conversation was tough for her to hear. Her favorite comeback was usually "Aw, girl ..." However, I continued the discussion. I finally confronted her about not believing my accusations of the abuser. I further shared my hurt regarding her not believing what the Pastor had told me to do, and how this impacted my life. My mom still struggled to accept what I was saying, but it got better because she tried. She did apologize to me. Although it was not easy for her, she did it.

As a result, our relationship moved to a better place. I wished we had greater healing, but it was good enough for me. Barriers in our relationship began to crumble. I no longer felt wounded by my mom. I was able to see her as a person who had her own childhood stories, hurts, pains and disappointments. I accepted that my mom reared me the best she knew how, and she loved me.

Forgiving My Dad

It was a shock for me to realize that I needed to forgive my dad. It was exhausting to have to forgive so much. I had come to realize that my dad did not protect me, as it relates to sexual abuse. I saw my dad as a hero who could not do anything wrong. Proverbs 16:11 states, "The Lord demands accurate scales and balances; he sets the standards for fairness" (NLT).

One particular night I had been sitting before the Lord, weary from crying. As I sat in my prayer corner, the process of healing was intense. The Lord spoke, stressing that I did not have an accurate opinion about my Dad. I couldn't believe what He was saying. I remember looking up to heaven, shaking my head, and bursting into tears. How could I have believed a lie about my dad? Was the Lord telling me that I believed in yet another lie? God began to pour into my spirit a better understanding of my dad. The scales of fairness were now balancing, and this was difficult to swallow. God enlightened me about how my dad was not perfect. He took me down memory lane and opened my eyes to the way my dad treated my mom. I realized that my father, at times, disrespected my mother and did not teach me to treat her with respect, either. Therefore, I became angry with my dad, and for a period of time I didn't visit my parents.

The Bible tells us in John 16:13, "But when he, the Spirit of truth, comes, he will guide you into all truth." The Word of God was being demonstrated in my life. The Holy Spirit was revealing truth to me. Eventually, my heart became forgiving toward God and my dad. The Lord melted my heart and grew me up. My girlfriend and I had a saying, "It's time to put on our big girl panties," so that is what I did. I no longer thought from a child's perspective, but a mature one. My dad was still everything to me. However, I had a balanced and realistic view of him then, thanks to God.

Deuteronomy 5:16 repeats the commandment stated in Exodus:

> Honor your father and mother, as the Lord your God has commanded you, so that you may live long and that it may go well with you in the land the Lord your God is giving you.

The Lord has placed me in this land of America. The way I honor my parents determines how life will go for me on the soil of America. How enlightening is that? This is the first commandment with a promise. What I have heard others say is, "You better honor your mother and father or life is going to be short-lived for you." However, the Word says that you will prosper in the land that God has given you if you honor your parents. When God instructed me to apologize, He was giving me the opportunity to be blessed. I moved out of the way and allowed God to perform what He had destined for me. I released myself from the curse of disrespect and dishonor that I had toward my mom. God was calling me to obedience and lining me up with His Word.

Forgiving the Abuser

> For if you forgive other people when they sin against you, your heavenly Father will also forgive you. But if you do not forgive others their sins, your Father will not forgive your sins. (Matthew 6:14-15)

I think the hardest part of the healing process was God walking me into all truth. I had no idea how easy it was to believe a lie. God showed me that we live in a world system of lies. I believed many lies. I believed lies about my mother, father, and my relationship with others. I had a lot of guilt, rejection and condemnation. What I believed about myself was also a lie. I know that the question of "Who Am I" was distorted by the sexual abuse and my environment.

When God started dealing with me about forgiving the perpetrator, it was overwhelming. How could God ask me to forgive him, after all he had done to me? He traumatized me! For years, I struggled with mental images of a little girl being raped. The most damning part of this was that I carried the guilt of the sexual abuse as if I had done this wrong. The mental images would come and go, and they always produced fear. To add salt to my wound, I discovered statistics revealing that those who are perpetrated against may likely become perpetrators themselves. That was hard to hear. I interpreted that as meaning once raped, a person would then become a rapist. This information only served as another tool of indictment against me.

God had to mature me to make me understand that simply because I was a victim, it did not mean that I was going to become a perpetrator. The Lord had to untwist all of this distortion and breathe truth into my life. Getting back to the little girl previously mentioned, the Lord opened my eyes and exposed me to the true meaning of those images. Because of God's power, enduring love and belief in me, I finally realized that the little girl in the vision was me.

One day I was listening to Dr. Charles Stanley, and he was preaching and expounding on forgiveness of others. He described a particular way to exercise forgiveness, and it stuck with me. The method was to take a chair for myself and one for the person who I needed to forgive. He further stated that I should begin to talk to the person as if they were sitting there. I thought this was quite crazy, but I was intrigued. That evening, I saw Dr. Sampson and asked his thoughts about it. He listened and gave me further instruction about what to do. He told me that I also needed to forgive that little girl within. So that evening when I got home, I did as instructed. I grabbed two chairs and invited God to help me through the process because I didn't know what to say. Dr. Stanley and Dr. Sampson had assured me that the words would flow. As I spoke to the perpetrator, the words did flow. I can't remember all that I said, but I gave him a piece of mind! I cried all through the process, poured out my heart, and then something amazing happened.

The Lord pressed in my spirit to get a picture of myself as a little girl. I found one and spoke to her. I told her that she was safe now and that it was not her fault. She had done a great job of caring for herself, and she deserved love. What happened to her was not love. That night, I no longer hated that little girl, but I accepted her. Before this, I spoke of myself in the third person, but it ended that night. I had experienced great freedom. God was doing a new thing in me, and I perceived it (Isaiah 43:19).

See, I am doing a new thing! Now it springs up; do you not perceive it? I am making a way in the wilderness and streams in the wasteland.

REFLECTION

I pray that you would allow God to shape you through all the pain and agony that you've suffered. If so, He will shape you into His intended purpose.

Then the word of the LORD came to me, saying: "O house of Israel, can I not do with you as this potter? says the LORD. "Look, as clay is in the potter's hand, so are you in My hand, O house of Israel!" (Jeremiah 18:5-6 NKJV)

~ *Reflections* ~
Write Your Thoughts

ELEVEN
My Journey

I am so grateful for my journey from darkness to light. It was an emotional journey from a stained dress to an unstained dress. When I think of the stained dress I can think of it metaphorically. The perpetrator's stain on my dress represented the pain, darkness and sorrow of the aftermath of abuse. God showed me the magnitude of the stain and its impact. My lack of knowledge and understanding of who I was in Christ would have permitted me to remain stained, but God had better plans for me. God would show me that I was loved, treasured, and adored, which was difficult to comprehend. The hurt kept me in captivity and blinded by darkness. But God, in His grace and mercy, did not allow me to stay in that state. He decided to deliver me and walk me through the process of understanding new life in Him.

Psalm 139:11-12 states,

If I say, 'Surely the darkness will hide me and the light become night around me,' even the darkness will not be dark to you; the night will shine like the day,for darkness is as light to you.

It is awesome to know that darkness cannot hide me. God's light is stronger, brighter and more than able to penetrate the darkness. As I drew near to God, God drew near to me (James 4:8). This verse didn't have a great deal of meaning until I started operating in that sphere of drawing near. As I positioned myself to get closer to God, the darkness that I struggled with could not stay. Darkness cannot compete with light ... think about it from this perspective: When you walk into a room and turn on the light, the darkness disappears. It is the same way with God. When we allow God to turn on the light in our lives, the darkness has to leave. However, we must also understand that it is a process.

"Wherever the hurt is, there lies the healing." I first heard a similar statement by Joyce Meyers, and it was my "aha!" moment, as Oprah Winfrey would say. I often found myself angry with God because it was difficult to choose healing, life and restoration when someone else caused the pain. How could God make me responsible for my own recovery? It seemed that the abuser was getting away with causing me pain. How could that be? This was a tough pill to swallow, but necessary. I had to make a conscious decision to get involved in the healing process or drown in my pains and sorrows. Over the years, I came to understand that I was not alone. I was talking to someone who was experiencing some tough times. She said to me that she was angry with God because she had to participate in her healing. She felt just as I did: She had not caused the pain, so why should she have to bear the burden of her own healing? She expressed that God had the ability to cause a change in her life instantly. I understood that wholeheartedly. I experienced similar struggles with God. I got so angry about the amount of emotional, mental, and spiritual work that I had to do. I would look at others and wonder why their lives seemed so simple. I also wondered in my heart why this had to happen to me. There was a time that I was so angry and frustrated with the process, that I just wanted to get in God's face and give Him a piece of my mind. I wanted the pain to end! As I was about to let loose my tirade of thoughts against God, the Lord took me to Psalm 73:21-28.

[21] When my heart was grieved and my spirit embittered,
[22] I was senseless and ignorant; I was a brute beast before you.
[23] Yet I am always with you; you hold me by my right hand.

^{24} You guide me with your counsel, and afterward you will take me into glory.
^{25} Whom have I in heaven but you? And earth has nothing I desire besides you.
^{26} My flesh and my heart may fail, but God is the strength of my heart and my portion forever.
^{27} Those who are far from you will perish; you destroy all who are unfaithful to you.
^{28} But as for me, it is good to be near God. I have made the Sovereign Lord my refuge; I will tell of all your deeds.

When I read this passage, I could not believe that I was reading these specific words in the Bible. David was expressing my deepest feelings. My heart softened, and I asked God to forgive me. He understood that my heart was grieved and embittered. Wow! He had heard it all before out of the mouth of David, and He could handle my feelings too. I also recalled Dr. Sampson preaching that David would start off expressing his feelings toward God and then shift to praising God. David acknowledged his feelings and understood that God was with Him, and God was with me too. The Lord was taking an opportunity to line up my thoughts and mind with His Word. I couldn't understand all that He was doing or why I had to go through this, but I had to choose God each time.

I had to choose what type of foundation I was going to lay for my life. I wanted a firm foundation, and I needed to get through what I was experiencing. I had to choose courage daily, and willingly follow the Word of God. I was building a firm foundation, and I learned that what I believed about myself could cause the foundation to either be strong or collapse.

REFLECTION

Why do you call me, 'Lord, Lord,' and do not do what I say? As for everyone who comes to me and hears my words and puts them into practice, I will show you what they are like. They are like a man building a house, who dug down deep and laid the foundation on rock. When a flood came, the torrent struck that house but could not shake it, because it was well built. But the one who hears my words and does not put them into practice is like a man who built a house on the ground without a foundation. The moment the torrent struck that house, it collapsed and its destruction was complete. (Luke 6:46-49)

~ *Reflections* ~
Write Your Thoughts

TWELVE
The Roots of Abuse

Genesis 34:1-5

Dinah and the Shechemites

[1] Now Dinah, the daughter Leah had borne to Jacob, went out to visit the women of the land.

[2] When Shechem son of Hamor the Hivite, the ruler of that area, saw her, he took her and raped her.

[3] His heart was drawn to Dinah the daughter of Jacob; he loved the young woman and spoke tenderly to her.

[4] And Shechem said to his father Hamor,"Get me this girl as my wife."

[5] When Jacob heard that his daughter Dinah had been defiled, his sons were in the fields with his livestock; so he did nothing about it until they came home.

I have read through the book of Genesis on numerous occasions, but for some reason, Dinah's rape never caught my eye, as it did this time. This chapter gives us an account of Dinah's rape. The Bible also enlightens us about both families' responses, or the lack thereof. The reader is left to ponder Dinah's response. It was surprising to learn that rape was specifically addressed in the Bible because I didn't think that God would include a story about rape in His Holy Word.

In Genesis 34, we embark upon the first mention of rape. The Bible tells us that Dinah was visiting the women of the land. Dinah was the only daughter of Jacob. Scholars believe that during this time, she was a teenager. The Bible does not specify if this was Dinah's first time visiting the women of the land or if she had visited multiple times. However, it is understandable that she may have wanted to mingle with other women. We learn that Shechem, then "saw her, took her and raped her."

Moses (the author of Genesis) tells us that Shechem's father was a ruler of that area and the country was of his namesake. We see that Shechem was a privileged and demanding young man (Genesis 34:4). Later, verse 19 describes him as the most honored of all his father's family. Additionally, we glean from the chapter that he is impulsive and self-seeking.

The chapter conveys that Shechem spoke tenderly to Dinah and he loved her. Wow! When you think about rape, you don't imagine the rapist speaking tenderly to and loving the victim. In my mind, this type of love is considered perverse at best. Nevertheless, let's focus on Shechem's tenderness for a moment. In the *New Strong's Exhaustive Concordance of The Bible*, the word love in Hebrew, *aw-hab'*, means to have affection for (sexually or otherwise). It is clear from the Scripture that Shechem had affection for Dinah, but it was sexual, as his conduct toward her indicates. Furthermore, the text also reveals that he spoke tenderly to her. We could assume that Shechem's actions, deeds, and words exhibited kindness and may have caused Dinah to feel confused. What is also revealing is that the only voice that we hear is his, not Dinah's.

I mentioned in an earlier chapter that the perpetrator spoke tenderly to me. He did not show anger or frustration toward me. He told me that he loved me and that he was going to marry me. He also kissed me tenderly. In my child-like mind, I was his Barbie, and he was my Ken. I can remember feeling strange about what he was saying and doing, but I did not know what to say. From the research I have done, it is common *not* to hear the voice of victims because the abuser silences them in many ways. In *The Trauma Myth*, the author explains that children are unable to process or make sense of sexually toned encounters. She further states that some later occurrence often triggers the abusive event. Her research findings indicate that most sexual violations are not violent or aggressive, because they occur with someone the children knew (Clancy, 37-38).

The National Sex Offender Public Website provides some statistical data on child/teen victims:

- In a 2012 maltreatment report, of the victims who were sexually abused, 26% were in the age group of 12–14 years and 34% were younger than 9 years.

- Approximately 1.8 million adolescents in the United States have been the victims of sexual assault.

- Research conducted by the Centers for Disease Control (CDC) estimates that approximately 1 in 6 boys and 1 in 4 girls are sexually abused before the age of 18.

- 35.8% of sexual assaults occur when the victim is between the ages of 12 and 17.

- 82% of all juvenile victims are female.

- 69% of the teen sexual assaults reported to law enforcement occurred in the residence of the victim, the offender, or another individual.

- Teens 16 to 19 years of age were 3 ½ times more likely than the general population to be victims of rape, attempted rape, or sexual assault.

- Approximately 1 in 5 female high school students report being physically and/or sexually abused by a dating partner.

So, not hearing Dinah's voice is not strange from an abuse standpoint. It is almost as if she is shut out of the ordeal, although it is happening to her. Because of the difference in their families' status, Dinah may have been at a loss about what to do. Shechem had no consideration for her wants, desires, feelings, or aspirations. He treated her as if she was an object that he needed to possess. He thought it perfectly fine to take a young girl that he did not know, rape her, and then demand that his father get her for his wife.

The subsequent interaction between the fathers is significant.

> [6.]Then Shechem's father Hamor went out to talk with Jacob. [7] Meanwhile, Jacob's sons had come in from the fields as soon as they heard what had happened. They were shocked and furious because Shechem had done an outrageous thing in Israel by sleeping with Jacob's daughter—a thing that should not be done.

I found this passage to be mind boggling, and its depth could easily be glossed over. There is so much that is unknown in the chapter, but one can speculate. For instance, if Hamor knew that his son had defiled another man's daughter, would he have willingly sought Jacob out? Or, since Hamor was a privileged man, would he have seen anything wrong with what his son had done? The Scripture does not reveal that Hamor had foreknowledge of the rape. It doesn't indicate how Jacob found out about it either, but we do learn that it was disturbing to him.

The two fathers met for the first time, and each experienced different emotions. Hamor may have been happy to ask for Jacob's daughter's hand in marriage on behalf of his son. That's sick, isn't it? Jacob, on the other hand, may have experienced confusion, apprehension, and disgust, while attempting to make sense out of what happened.

Conversely, Jacob could have felt that Hamor was coming to make amends for what his son had done. He could have also felt that Shechem marrying his daughter was the decent thing to do, considering the circumstances. This is addressed in Deuteronomy 22:28-29.

> If a man happens to meet a virgin who is not pledged to be married and rapes her and they are discovered, he shall pay her father fifty shekels of silver. He must marry the young

woman, for he has violated her. He can never divorce her as long as he lives.

You may find this law distasteful, and for us in this day and time, it is. But it was a law put in place to deal with the violator during ancient times. Furthermore, this law was not in place when Dinah was raped, but it was viewed as an act of defilement against Dinah and Israel.

What I will discuss next excites my emotions but may be appalling to some. First, allow me to admit that Jacob's sons are my heroes. Verse 7 reads, "Meanwhile, Jacob's sons had come in from the fields as soon as they heard what had happened. They were shocked and furious because Shechem had done an outrageous thing in Israel by sleeping with Jacob's daughter— a thing that should not be done."

Now let's closely examine the brothers' reaction. What happened to their sister was tragic, and it aroused strong, raw emotions in them. The passage revealed that her brothers were shocked and furious. Dictionary.com describes *shock* as "a sudden and violent blow or impact; collision." The word *furious* is defined as "full of fury, violent passion, or rage; extremely angry; enraged." What the Bible appears to say is that when the brothers heard the news, it was like a great force came against them. It further communicated that while being struck with such a great force of violence, the brothers were also filled with violent anger, and/or rage. In the New Revised Standard Version, verse 7 says that the men were "indignant and very angry."

I love their reaction. These brothers were deeply impacted by the tragedy their sister endured. Think of her brothers' anger from the perspective of road rage. We hear many stories of people becoming enraged over someone cutting them off while driving or damaging their car. However, the impact upon sexually violated children may not cause outrage. In contrast, two of Dinah's brothers plotted against Shechem and his father, with the intention of exacting justice for the heinous act.

I have spoken with women whose family members were aware of what happened to them, and yet did nothing. More specifically, these victims said that no one paused to share in their pain. This revelation is quite disturbing. Why aren't more families outraged, angered, and furious? I know that there are those who have stood up and rescued their relatives from the clutches of perpetrators. However, if there is one victim who is not rescued, then that is one too many. It's understandable that there may be various reasons why families may fail to intervene: fear, lack of knowledge and understanding, disbelief, financial dependence, or maybe they were victims themselves. Many females have been raped or molested and have never told anyone. They continue to live with this horrible crime in silence.

Dinah's brothers were outraged because the rape should not have happened. I find these words to be lifesaving: *It should not have been done.* Her brothers didn't think that she had done something wrong. They put the entire responsibility on the shoulders of Shechem. He was the one to blame. The brothers were so infuriated that two of them killed Shechem, his father, and every man in the land. Although their response was drastic, they responded.

It helped my healing process to share my experience with some members of my family. I shared with a cousin, who has gone on to be with the Lord. I tearfully told him what happened. To my surprise, he revealed that he and my brother discovered what the perpetrator had done, and they jumped him. I was stunned. My tears immediately stopped flowing. This made me feel so loved to know that my family had sought to protect me! I truly believe that God allowed me to connect with my cousin that day so I could have some relief. Thank you, Jesus! My brother couldn't tell me what he had done to protect me because tragically, he was killed when I was twelve years old. Later, I realized that the abuse stopped at some point, and this could have been due to my family's intervention. As I had previously shared, there were still incidents when he attempted to harass me verbally, but the sexual coercion stopped.

~ Reflections ~
Write Your Thoughts

Sisters, Raise Your Voices!
Final Reflection

As I worked on the finishing touches of my book, I watched the Michigan Circuit Court proceedings with intensity and at times found my eyes glued on the trusted doctor, Larry Nassar. He was a pillar of the gymnastics and Olympic community, now prosecuted for sexually abusing over 150 young female gymnasts. He, like so many other predators, thought he had silenced the voices of these young ladies. However, their voices were heard loudly and clearly by the world, as they poured out their heart-wrenching testimonies of the abuse they endured. Judge Rosemarie Aquiline had given the young ladies an unprecedented opportunity to express the pain and agony they suffered at his hand.

At times, it became difficult to listen to them bare their emotions and vulnerability before us. It was interesting to observe Larry Nassar's disposition. What struck me, was noting his frailty and weakness. He was no longer the powerful and admired doctor. The tide had turned, and the young ladies were seen as empowered, courageous, and brave. He was now viewed as a disgusting pervert, who would spend the rest of his life in prison.

These young ladies potentially gave voice to every young girl, teen, and woman who suffered sexual abuse. I pray that many more young ladies will find their voices and never live in silence again. My hope is that as voices rise, they will be heard. Many females will be released from shame, guilt, dirtiness, and fault. As the voices rise, healing and restoration may happen simultaneously throughout the world.

One way to facilitate that change is by women of all ages taking up arms within the community. Becoming the watchmen on the wall will provide a safe haven for other girls, young ladies and women to heal. I encourage all sisters who would like to get involved to contact me at my information below:

Regina C Hall
Enlighten Heart Services, LLC
sistersjourneyingtogether@gmail.com

AFTERWORD ...
AND A PRAYER

Men, they need us now more than ever.

Having been blessed to be a male midwife in the creation of this powerful work that is in your hands, I can honestly say that I have been convicted—figuratively and literally—to heed the clarion call embodied in those words.

Men, they need us now more than ever.

Appropriate words. Necessary words. Words that are the logical segue from the heart-wrenching words of the title of this book, *Mommy, I Need You!*

For us men, we are needed now more than ever. We are needed to be present, to be there as watchmen, as protectors, as able brothers, fathers, grandfathers, and uncles ... and friends. We are being called to make amends with the traumas that made so many of us take on directions and actions in life that created horrible sexual legacies in our communities. So many of us have our own stories of being sexually abused or worse, and in having been such, we function with distorted, greatly maligned self-images of who we are as sexual beings. We need to be who God created us to be.

That, however, is going to take some work.

Inculcation of imbalanced ideas and perspectives about females and how to relate to them sexually begins early for many of us. A well-intentioned uncle who wants us to be savvy in the ways of romance introduces pornography to us during those early impressionable years of our life. A doting single mother infuses in us the attributes of being a womanizer out of fear not doing so will lead to homosexuality. An admired leader of a regular gathering of "the guys" spins spellbinding tales of his numerous sexual conquests, tales that are often much more fiction than fact.

By the time we come of age sexually, we are an ungodly force to be reckoned with. Filled to the brim with bad intentions for all the right reasons (at least, that is what we are erroneously told by the world and by many of our well-intentioned elders), we go forth and live out yet another in a long line of generational curses.

Yes, we can blame Adam.

To paraphrase Genesis in the passage where God confronts the couple about their transgression in eating the forbidden fruit, *it was that woman you gave me who made me do this*.

What we know to be true, however, are two essential things:

God created Adam first.

If Adam, having been approached by Eve to share in the fruit, had simply said, "Let's check with God first," all of us would be living a different reality today.

Men, they need us now more than ever.

The Second Adam, Jesus Christ, through the sacrifice on the cross, created the way to restoration with God, to become-- to BE--the sons of God we were meant to be. In this sense, for us men, the need for salvation in Christ Jesus is as much a need to save our souls as it is to lay claim upon our true self-image as Men of God.

What I am speaking of came forth as an unintended consequence resulting from my having the opportunity to serve as a help-meet in the creation of this book. Yes, I am intentionally using female-related terms—*help-meet*, and earlier, *midwife*—to make my points here. I do so to make this final point: There is much about being men that we can learn from fully embracing and reflecting upon the sexual traumas of women and humbling ourselves in the process. We all need to be convicted, convicted well and convicted deeply, so that we can find better ways to be better Men of God.

If we do, our Women of God—and our communities, and the continual efforts to build God's kingdom on earth—will truly flourish.

Thank you, Regina, for your sacrifice and courage, and for your obedience to the Holy Spirit.

Amen.

Dr. Robert McTyre
Author of *The New Male Voice*

REFERENCES

Clancy, Susan. 2011. *The Trauma Myth: The Truth About the Sexual Abuse of Children – and Its Aftermath*. New York: Basic Books.

Dictionary.com. n.d. "Desolate." Accessed March 25, 2018. http://www.dictionary.com/browse/desolate.

_____. n.d. "Innocence." Accessed March 25, 2018. http://www.dictionary.com /browse/innocence.

Erickson, Erik. 2017. "Erik Erickson's Eight Stages of Psychosocial Development." http://web.cortland.edu /andersmd/ERIK/sum.HTML.

Got Questions. 2016. "Why Did Amnon Rape Tamar? Why Didn't David Punish Amnon?" https://gotquestions.org/ Amnon-and-Tamar.html.

Michigan Department of Health and Human Services. n.d. "A Parent's Guide to Working with Children's Protective Services." http://www.michigan.gov/mdhhs/0,5885,7-339-73971_7119_25045---,00.html.

Michigan Legislature. 1975. "Child Protection Law Act 238 of 1975." 722.622 Definitions. Sec. 2 (g) and (z). http://www.legislature.mi.gov/(S(wwn5twmaq0tva1o0vi1u kb2g))/mileg.aspx?page=getObject&objectName=mcl-722-622.

_____. 2008. "The Michigan Penal Code Act of 1931." 750.520a. Sec. 520a Amended Definitions (q) and (r) .

REFERENCES

http://www.legislature.mi.gov/documents/mcl/pdf/mcl-750-520a-amended.pdf.

Project Sakinah. n.d. "Defining Child Sexual Abuse." http://projectsakinah.org/Family-Violence/Child-Abuse/Child-Sexual-Abuse.

U.S. Department of Justice National Sex Offenders Public Website. n.d. "Facts and Statistics." https://www.nsopw.gov/en/education/factsstatistics/.

Vocabulary.com. n.d. "Parasitic." Accessed March 25, 2018. https://www.vocabulary.com/dictionary/parasitc.

Wikipedia contributors. 2018. "Sexual Identity." In *Wikipedia, The Free Encyclopedia*. Accessed March 23, 2018. https://en.wikipedia.org/w/index.php?title =Sexual _identity&oldid=823283127.

Made in the USA
Columbia, SC
25 September 2019